Defending Darkness

OTHER BOOKS BY
PAMELA PORTER

House Made of Rain
(Ronsdale Press, 2014)

Late Moon (Ronsdale Press, 2013)

No Ordinary Place (Ronsdale Press, 2012)

I'll Be Watching (Groundwood Books, 2011)

This Awakening to Light (Leaf Press, 2010)

Cathedral (Ronsdale Press, 2010)

The Intelligence of Animals
(Backwaters Press, 2008)

Yellow Moon, Apple Moon
(Groundwood Books, 2008)

Stones Call Out (Coteau Books, 2006)

The Crazy Man (Groundwood Books, 2005)

Sky (Groundwood Books, 2004)

Poems for the Luminous World
(Frog Hollow Press, 2002)

defending darkness

Pamela Porter

RONSDALE

RONSDALE PRESS
3350 West 21st Avenue
Vancouver, B.C., Canada V6S 1G7
www.ronsdalepress.com

Typesetting: Julie Cochrane, in New Baskerville 11 pt on 13.5
Cover Design: Julie Cochrane
Paper: Enviro 100 Edition, 55 lb. Antique Cream (FSC) — 100%
    post-consumer waste, totally chlorine-free and acid-free

Ronsdale Press wishes to thank the following for their support of its publishing program: the Canada Council for the Arts, the Government of Canada through the Canada Book Fund, the British Columbia Arts Council, and the Province of British Columbia through the Book Publishing Tax Credit Program.

Library and Archives Canada Cataloguing in Publication

Porter, Pamela, 1956–, author
    Defending darkness / Pamela Porter.

Poems.
Issued in print and electronic formats.
ISBN 978-1-55380-470-3 (print)
ISBN 978-1-55380-471-0 (ebook) / ISBN 978-1-55380-472-7 (pdf)

    I. Title.

PS8581.O7573D44 2016   C811'.6   C2016-902109-2   C2016-902110-6

Printed in Canada by Marquis Book Printing, Quebec

for Rob, Cecilia and Drew

always and forever remember my love

ACKNOWLEDGEMENTS

Grateful acknowledgement is made to the following publications in which poems in this book first appeared:

CBC – Canada Writes, Cede Poetry, Coastal Spectator, Literary Review of Canada, Our Times, Vallum, WordWorks.

"Borealis" was a finalist for the 2013 CBC Canada Writes Poetry Prize.

"Albion mine, 1918" won the 2014 Lena Endicott Poetry Prize for a political poem.

"None so prized" appeared in the Coast Collective Gallery's exhibit, *Poets Speak, Artists Respond*, September 2015.

"How to disappear" appeared in the Art Gallery of Greater Victoria's *In Another Place, and Here*, April 2015.

"Admonition," "Directive for Holiness," "Harvest," "Hilda," "In Ordinary Time," and "When the Wild Horse Spoke" appeared in chapbooks edited by Patrick Lane, published by Leaf Press.

My thanks and appreciation go to Ron Hatch and all at Ronsdale Press for your faithful and careful work, your patience, and your high standards. Also, I wish to express my gratitude to Russell Thorburn for lending your gifts and wise advice to this book and all the others. My gratitude as well goes to the community of poets at Planet Earth Poetry and the Honeymoon Bay retreats for your support, kindness and inspiration. And, as always, to my family, for your constant love.

NOTES

"Hilda": Allis Chalmers was a brand of farm tractor widely used in North America until the 1980s.

"Virga": Virga is a term used to describe wisps of precipitation which evaporate before reaching the ground.

"Bottle tree": a bottle tree is a small tree usually no longer alive, on which glass bottles are set on the ends of branches to keep away evil spirits.

"The fires": "lion" refers to a mountain lion, also known as cougar.

"The way things separate": The Flathead river originates in the Canadian Rockies and flows southwest into Flathead Lake in Montana, then empties into the Clark Fork River.

"Maddybenny Farm" is located in Northern Ireland.

CONTENTS

– I –

To own nothing, not even our skin

To live here
beneath cedars and firs.
To live among osprey, raven, peregrine, owl.
To feel the sun grow colder,
night more eager to arrive.
To close the barn's red mouth, the cats inside.
To come in from the horses.
To warm the hands. And with
warm hands, to sit at the piano,
teach the hands a new pattern.
Something labyrinthine for the left.
Something with trills for the right.
To watch the mind and hands work together.
To do this with sunlight between the tips
of two trees, and light falling into the room, light
that started on the sun now grazing the page,
black notes on white paper.
To recognize beauty if not to understand it.
To go out to the horses again,
bring them in from the field, lay
my hands on their foreheads, necks, withers.
To learn the music of them.
To know, then, that this life is all one day.
A day in which quail break out of their eggs
and scurry in single file across the yard.
A day in which dandelions bloom and hurl
their seeds to the wind,
and the great heart of the world
grants the air its breath.
To live to eat and drink some piece of the day.
To say, where are we
but on the floor of a vast ocean,
blinking and blinking our eyes
as light breaks through the blue above us.

Directive for holiness

after Miłosz

A woman with child should not walk on dry twigs in spring.
Should she dream of horses running in moonlight,
                                        her labour will be quick.
Her husband should not carry an axe into the house.
A son should not slice an apple in two but a daughter should
do so, and count the seeds which will number her children.
A man should not kill a lynx in snow nor let the blood
                                        drip a path to his door.
If he does so, his wife must cover the blood with bark or leaves
or river stones, else it will bring injury or death into the house.
This I learned from the snake handlers who lived in the coulee,
who mark misfortune in lightning-split trees, dust swept up
by brooms, a girl's first blood.

The abandoned farm

You wake to mottled light and know you've gone there again:
the strip-log house, the well run dry, and wind spilling
through broken windows, and sagging fence wire tangled
in sheep's wool still whistling drought stories down the valley.
All through summer and the slow death of flowers, the cat's
litter of six would tumble over themselves in wild grass, carried
off in talons one after another; that, and the pine bed

where your children slippered out matted, bruised, but for one
who turned back, and no stone ever laid for her that lay buried
months in snow, nor the stained sheets he rolled over and over
his arms and threw away, that could prove her real. Twenty
years scouring your dreams and the blackened edges of fields
for something wild like her to look you in the eye, circle
at a distance like coyotes for sheep.

Then June would open its green eyes, the neighbour
in his truck who aimed his head out the window, his front
tire careful over the rattler's blunt head, too close to the house
to let it live. One knife stroke severed the rattle he curled into
your son's pink palm. Your man's cupped hands overflowed
with mustard in bloom, the way
he'd unbutton your blouse, slow, deliberate,

and taught you to mend fence, wind wires over each other
not even the horses could break through, how you'd think
of yourself then as a child in school, pencil in the wrong hand
writing *o* and *o* and *o*, she with hair flaming, still a child
in you, sometimes slides, silent, out, while you squint high
into the pine and see her there. *Come, down, child,*
come down, you call,
> *I will show you no more.*

Like sunlight carried on the current

A stranger light has entered me
and made my veins shine as dawn
on all the tributaries of a river.
A stranger light, a brighter dark.
Where has it come from? For its tenor
is not of this world. Where will it go,
if I am not its ending place?
A train passes field after field of wheat,
its steel howl which the coyote answers
from a distant hill. Tonight I listen to rain,
wind in the wide valleys, my veins
flowing into each other beneath
the caul of my skin. Unlike the china cup
shattered and mended with gold,
I am not prized, but sometimes
noticed by the moon
in whose watery light she washes
the dust of dying stars from her face.

Aubade

A slight, slant snow, *a good day for burning*, he said, the land
coveted for growing. Then he surrounded the farmhouse
with kerosene, though I'd made him wait holding the match
while I searched its rooms, and emerged carrying a locket,
a Bible with flowers pressed in the Psalms, oars
in their oarlocks, a newspaper from my birth year
stuffed into the basement joists. The house a conflagration,
burned as though taken up by heaven. Bats fled the rooms
and rose like daylight stars; a scrap of wallpaper floated
toward the ground. The heat of it singed our faces, melted
the snow. And the next summer, drove to the place again,
three days sleeping in the open under a net.
I wakened to a fox calling somewhere in the slow
curved distance, then silence, then answer: a loon alone
by the dock, though we'd slept on after our love, the night
too warm, both our nakedness free for the air to do with us
what it wanted. And home, and he flown to the other side
of the world. I found a dark hair left on his pillow like a road
half-covered in snow, and kept it there, as though it were
a letter whose words, no matter how rearranged, are a sadness,
a grief. And so pure a grief it was, that stillness on one side
of the bed, the light falling into the dark. I would tell him,
his voice far and small through the phone, how I saw a mouse
take flight in the talons of an owl, the ploughed field take on
the idea of absence, and then the owl, two notes of boast,
two of regret. Those nights, waiting for sleep, I listened
for the lap of his boat rowing back, the same ghostly sound
the deer make when they run through the stream, the night
fanning out in circles, his oars' wide wings.

Divining

When the book wore out, she buried it like a cat,
and buried the words, too, in her heart, the way
they arranged themselves on the page like lovers —
how *the memory of snow dusting his shoulders*
would always be held by *when she carried his ashes in a bowl.*
She wondered if someone someday, digging a garden beside
the house might uncover the earth-stained broken spine,
the shovel, blind mole, knocking against it like a stone.
Dawn, bare trees filling themselves with light,
she noticed how the rose, ravished by night's rain,
lay fallen like a shattered moon, and remembered
how in early spring she'd watched the thin-bladed moonrise,
snow still clinging in low places, how she wanted to slip
onto the back of the sorrel paint grazing the frail grass,
drive him with only her legs and quiet words down the valley
following the river; how she believed something she'd lost
still lay hidden in the world, waiting for her; how, listening,
she could hear birds mating all over the Chilcotin.

Endurance

In the mirror was an open window and billowing curtains,
a moth, a small darkness climbing the glass.
She sat down on a wood floor with paper and pastels
and began to draw memory, dust in the corners of the room
and how the dying sun, the sky behind naked trees
smeared her hands, her fingers turned the colour of grief.
And she drew the girl who lived inside her, dusk and the trees
burnt-black, the highest branches a map of her veins.
A soul inside a body, and the body a gathering of scars
from years searching for her lover and her children
not yet born, her clothing torn on fence wire
and broken ice on the river where her foot went through,
her despair so large she once lay down to die,
but death turned its back and she slept, curled on pine boughs,
dreaming herself under the ice and their hands
just beyond her grasp. Years later she'd cross a border
between countries, to a house hidden under pines,
a scattering of feathers on the windowsill where a moth
climbed the glass, a planet so distant she could make out
only a brief darkness in a mirror. And she thought
of afternoon, the field, the air she could almost see
swirling under clouds moving down from the north,
blackbirds rising like leaves blown higher and higher.
Beneath the ground where she stood lay the bones of horses
whose spirits she sometimes saw grazing the quiet grass.
Then she would turn her stained hands toward the sky and say,
Like light that survives the fall through great trees am I,
her hair copper in the autumn wind,
her feet holding to stony ground.

Turn and counter-turn

At the end she was left with two horses, barn cats
and a rabbit. By then she had grown smaller
and more distant, as though the world watched her
through the wide end of a telescope.
And resembled Cordelia, who waited all that time
for Lear to notice his mistake.
The damage was done and then
her bones healed wrong, like the ones
she stroked as a child, sun-paled on the desert floor
below cliffs striated with light. How fragile
the venomous — the skeleton, a rattler,
its impression in the sand incremental, a fossil's birth.
There are still things that do not die:
stone, iron given up by earth, the heart's expectations.
Some chiselled by wind, some born by fire.
Some so delicate they fall open like a flower.

Albion mine, 1918

Four days after the explosion,
a few of the men descended, caged
and raised to ground the remaining ones,
a dozen or so, and at the noon horn,
the pit ponies,
harnessed each to a carriage,
passed one and by one beneath the iron gates,
through the exhausted town, to church,
and halted, the strange snow
clinging to their hooves. And with half-
blind eyes, blinked back
the coal-grey light.
And stood, mane-less, tail-less, thus obedient
while the organ gasped and sang,
and boots shuffled over the wooden floor.

Next dawn
the new boys with school lunch pails
wait in a row, in place of their fathers,
to see who will be given the bay, the paint,
their soiled plainness,
the men's coal-creased hands
handing over each frayed and knotted rope.

Both boy and pony
lurch as the cage doors boom shut,
together going down into the dark.

All they could do

The dead, they've gone wild, every last one,
teeming the rivers, rainbow, golden,
swum backwards into time, breathing underwater
as the living can only in dream.
And watch us from the edge of the wood, beyond grief,
camouflaged leaf-shadow grey, blended in
with rain. Cloven tracks we've found mornings,
circling the house as we slept caged in our beds.
Our dead arrive, congregants at the feeder,
cacophonous heavenly choir, wing-striped, crested,
rewarded for a lifetime loving us, sacrificial.
Nonetheless, we call to them who do not answer,
who made us who we are, their eyes in the urgent dark,
something they need to tell us, have come all this way
through the night with her starry teeth,
lips sewn shut, forbidden to speak.
With sky our witness, the snow laid like a garment
stained, trivial, left behind, the stone rolled away.
We'll wait months, years even, ride the clock's
slow hands around, winter to summer till they come again,
here where we always were, grown older,
the tiny tin bells of our hearts rusted quiet.
Still, some indigo, raven or crow, sets to rocking
the highest branches; others ride thermals, circular,
alone or in pairs higher toward eternity.
They've found us broken, our throats grief-clotted,
they've held the air in their fists.
All they could do to bring the message,
to touch us in that place beyond speech.

Moving horses to high country

They have gone now to join the others —
the wild, the Chilcotin, leaf and twig woven into their manes,
nostrils wide as blackened moons. I, too, rode them out
on the mare's wide back, past a cluster of aspen,
cloistered monks of the plateau. And the monks
nodded with the tips of their hoods, and the horses — the wild,
the Chilcotin — blew through their nostrils
at the sight of us riding the backs of the tame.
And when night comes to the high places, the stars
gather in great herds, they lie down among the warmth
of each other on the indigo plain. They have gone,
the tame, joined to the wild until the snows, the wind
chasing after them, with hooves flying, and flown.

In from the sea

Each day I ask less and less of the world,
and waken each morning a child, and spend my days
studying the writings of horses, their cuneiform
pressed into damp ground,
                    how the ideogram for confidence
                            is *raven on the barn roof*;
and for bewildered, *pines blurred with mist.*
How the creek goes on with her stories so shyly
the horses must bend their necks to listen.
Once he said of them,
                    such huge hearts to care for,
before he went silent as a stone god, and the sky
hung down in every direction, and the night
extinguished all her torches,
which, incidentally, is the ideogram for death:
                            a darkness without stars.
So, we will turn to ash. Or be swallowed by the earth.
Even now death holds the moon hostage
                    before she wings her escape
by growing thin as light behind a door.

There are days I wait hard for something to happen.
For the firs to stitch their histories to the wind.
For spiders to pull the fog in from the sea
                            with their nets.
For sleep (*the sea in which we drown*) to say,
                    yes, but my time is short.

Guatemala

Her horses stood grazing on the graves of the old ones
and swivelled their ears at the sound of her walking
through leaves wide enough to write on. She thought
of the medicine woman who taught her to send letters
to the dead on thin papers strung across the creek
between branches of slender maples, the prolifery of ferns.
All winter she dreamed them rising like sparrows, alighted
on the firs where owls once mated, how she waited each night
for the owls' soft cries, but heard only absence and the silences
of moss. She stood with the horses on the graves
of the old ones and remembered a plaza in the days
after the massacre, men whispering beneath their hats,
women setting plastic flowers in the dirt, and the woman
with hair the colour of ravens, who spoke to her in a tongue
not her own, the woman waving her hands, dried mud
pale around her fingernails, asking her, *Entiendes?*
Do you understand? In her mind were the maples
she returned to in spring, the letters gone,
webbed string lifting in wind. And the owls. Where
were the owls? The woman's hands held her.
The woman's hands. *Entiendes?* And though she did not,
nodded and nodded her head, *Sí, sí, sí.*

Harvest

And no way now to know what happened then, only
that it did, with ropes of geese knotting up the sky
and wind-strained clouds riding the skin of that river.
You might have said, *soon the day will shatter,*
but no one ever does, not even the ones who pray,
Just this once let me know how it turns out.
Never mind. We find out soon enough. Truth is,
they went hours thinking he was with someone else.
The combines working through the night with their great lamps,
getting the grain off before the snow, long past the sun's
slow fire burning out. And no one can say how
he got up there, high inside the silo, twelve years old,
another mother's son. Something swung wrong
and knocked him in. Like the sea that erases everything.
And finally near dawn, drained the silo, grain rising
in mountains when he poured out, grain falling
from his mouth, his ears, and no one with the book
open to the page, to speak the words
      We brought nothing into this world,
      and we can carry nothing out.
      The Lord gave, and the Lord hath taken away,
their hands dangled at their sides, everyone standing around
as they would at a birth, the moon settling its light on them all,
the wind so fierce it shook the stars.

You said

After the curtains billowed into the room
and the spider anchored the last corner with her silk
and the pond broke its icy silence
and the ferns loosed their tight-curled new born;
after the day hung a little longer in the sky
and the hills pulled on their dark robes
and one planet mirrored the departing light
and then another, you said, *Now.*
And it was now. And still. And still.

The first musicians were birds

As you can see, the music is not difficult;
it is a very simple piece.
The difficulty lies, for the pianist,
in making the notes sing.
To do so, the music must be born
deep within the body, ascend into the heart
and exit through the hands,
as a meadowlark on a fence post
reaches into the heart of the earth
with the pale roots, her feet,
so that the song may fly from her beak.
Thus when approaching the music,
we must remember:
it is that simple. Be the bird.

It was a kind of worship

In the years when there was only silence between them,
she spent her days speaking with horses, and the feral cats
who claimed the creek and underbrush as their country.
She exchanged letters with the maples, read poetry aloud
to the grass. When he saw her again, there was a wildness
in her, and a light wrapped about her like a scarf
made of the moon's reflection on the sea. Protection
for the nights when death stalked her with such stealth
that its eyes were all she saw of it in the dark.
Because of a dream, she knew to expect him once the trees
called the sun to warm their nakedness, and when
he appeared, she led him to the deer's nesting place.
And the deer spoke to him from their eyes, *You
are no predator. Even so, we will hold our children close.*
And the stars, hearing, came forth one by one.
Later, as an old man, he would remember this about her,
how the moon sang all the ancient songs, and the pines
lay their blankets on the ground, and the darkness chanted,
You do not know me. Never will you know me.

Woman at the piano

So much goes unpraised: thorns, rust, the burned house
vacant but for a piano out of tune. She sits down,
spreads her fingers and begins to play,
the music made giant by the floors and walls
until she lifts her hands and folds them in her lap
the way the spirit does when it has given up,
and asks only for quiet, and for the windows,
dusk without a moon. In the orchard, two deer
stand at attention, their skin quivering
in small, quick ripples, the only music they'd known
until this moment having been a choir of bees
carving cathedrals into the fallen pears.

– II –

Lilacs

I knew then what was required —
that I must carry the rest of the story.
You could say I was an instrument of music,
a keeper of accounts: rain, the charting of light,
what bones the ravens discarded
in the horses' trough. Everything
has led to this: a sorrow rolled in, an undertow.
The stone that the builder rejected.
And so I became keeper of the lilacs
for one brief season.
To cradle in both my hands a heart,
fragrant and wanting. A lantern, each one.
For this I was born; for lilacs, thus endowed.
Mornings I found them humming
with desire and bees, passionate, a heart
that accepts all the love offered,
like infants who've never been betrayed.
For that moment we were, the lilacs and I,
holy and acceptable.
But too soon faded, dulled, skeletal,
the blossoms flown as ash, condemned
to ride the winter drained of colour,
far as you could see as the day lay down.
As all my beloved dying at once,
their lives abandoned as ships flung on rocks.
There was music Mozart never finished.
Those days I'd hear it just before waking,
winged insects beating the glass, that thin
passage bridging the dark
divided continents of the brain.
Still, I knew my hardship — to carry
the rest of the story, grief that lay between death
and its opposite, the long road back to lilacs again.

As if I hoisted the moon nightly in my arms
to begin again, reborn. You could say
we were instruments of music, every one,
that we sang for a season.
We whose season is brief, must carry all we can.

The mind wants to know

Take away the rain,
the rain-tipped blades of grass,

take away the human print pressed like a fossil
into earth, and the heart's improbable dreaming.

What will you have then?

Darkness, and the wild maple's storm,
flocks of clouds moving on,

and stars with their cold closed mouths.

But the heart reaches deep into memory:
dawn, and the delicate bones of the wrist;

there was noon, she whispers, *there was breath*,
the heart's touch arriving moments before the flesh.

Heart, which moves in and out of this world.
Though the body has its limits, the heart has none.

Out of this, longing is born: snow geese
over the house, over the pines, calling;

far into the night, across the bereaved distances,
the blind heart's ears fall open

like a gate, a seam, like blossom, like wings.

Like a gate, a seam, like blossom, like wings,
the blind heart's ears fall open

across the bereaved distances,
far into the night,

over the house, over the pines, calling;
snow geese: out of this, longing is born.

Though the body has its limits, the heart has none.
Heart, which moves in and out of this world.

And the heart's touch, arriving
moments before the flesh.

There was noon, she whispers, *there was breath*;
dawn, and the delicate bones of the wrist.

Heart reaches deep into memory:
stars with their cold, closed mouths,

flocks of clouds moving on
and the wild maple's storm.

What will you have then?

Take away the heart's improbable dreaming,
and the human print pressed like a fossil into earth;

take away the rain, and the rain-tipped blades of grass.
The mind wants to know.

Mosaic

Morning. Upstairs on the main floor someone plays the organ,
a melody fragmented, paused, then re-started winds among us
in the room. Downstairs, the kitchen is alive with preparation
and the scent of soup and bread. Each day I worry
if my students have eaten, so I place on the table muffins —
blueberry — a mountain range between us. I must invite them
to partake, or my students will not eat. As we taste we talk
of fruits: American, Asian, the fruits of Laos. *Lychee,*
say the twin girls. *Lychee,* the old monk agrees, and the boy
who washes his car fresh every morning; all smile, nod,
as if the word, *lychee,* were a benediction. *We had lychee
in the prison camp,* says Dr. Saefong. *It grew on trees,*
and because today is his day to speak, he goes on: *they came
for me at my clinic. My wife and children did not know.
Four years, they knew nothing of me,* and I remember
the mosaic on the temple wall at Vientiane, a figure
in a sapphire shirt bent forward, intent, the path before him
rising into the mountains, the mosaic five hundred years old.
Anyone can see he is not a traveller; he carries no lantern,
no walking stick. He has slipped past the guards in the night
and is going into exile, the mountains looming over him,
a thin shard of moon. He cannot change his mind, cannot
choose another route. His path is set in stone. And when
he reaches the mountaintop and looks beyond
to the thread of river below, only now can we see
that the figure is Dr. Saefong, his shirt, trousers torn,
that the rains have begun, the storm bearing down
in a portion of the sky, and below, the river he must cross,
swollen, fast. He has no coins to pay his passage. The riverbank
is riddled with soldiers, thieves. To cross is impossible.
Yet he is here, at the table in the windowless room, the music
stopped, all silent but for his voice and his wife's quiet crying

beside him, because he is stumbling now toward the tent city
where she waits without hope, has given him up for dead,
and when he enters the camp he will fall to the ground, and she
will hardly recognize him. *It grew on trees,* he says, *lychee,*
as if it were a benediction.

In the before-time

Of my earliest memories is the prairie wolf, my first mother,
the butte and its tall grass plateau my home. How I came
to suckle from her, to be one with her litter, sleep with her
wolfen fur in my fists, is mystery. This, in the before-time.
Before I was taken away to a human mother. And through
this clarity, much is explained: the way I lean, listening,
for a high, distant singing, and of my instinct for the languages
of the great grass herds, and their wind-blown manes, and their
sibilant poetry. A human orderliness did not keep company
with me. A dog-shaped shadow I followed to the clean edge,
churned ocean of sky. And slept with my clan inside the earth,
all stilled paws and breath. And learned to watch the eyes
before all speech. To smell fear. That the Sabbath is evening,
blood-wash on the far hills, the hour between hawk and owl,
the moment for praise. One morning a cattleman climbed
the butte. Startled, and thinking me in danger, he raised
his rifle, murdering all but me. And carried me over the edge
into the world. Thus I was given to my human mother, who
frightened me when she drew her lips away from her teeth.
Who tasted a wildness on my skin. Who combed my hair,
dressed and shod me, and carried me to church. But I knew
the hour was wrong. Now, small creatures arrive at my door.
Wounded or ill, they die in my hands. I place them
in minute graves beneath the fir, while the wind
nuzzles the turned earth with her breath.

Borealis

The baby fevered on her lap, she watched the doctor's mouth
say *pneumonia,* say *hospital,* and stared at him as though
the words were foreign and she had to search her mind
for their meaning, the doctor saying after a silence that hospital
might be easier with her alone out there on the farm, but she
was thinking of the storm, how the water in the horses' trough
would have frozen by now, and she'd have to carry the enamel
pot across the snow, her hands in oven mitts, the water
steaming in the pot and her trying not to spill until she reached
the corral and poured the water in a rush over the rough ice,
the ice melting in the middle, leaving an edge of fine, scalloped
lace around the inside of the trough. And the sheep — shutting
them in the barn would be enough, but who knew what
it was like out there now: first wind, then dust, then leaves,
as she drove with the baby into town, then snow, horizontal,
bleaching the fields, the air, and she looked into the doctor's
eyes, who seemed genuinely sorry for her, and whispered
in her mind, *how did I think I could ever be a mother,*
but told the doctor she'd take the baby home, and he only
nodded his head, the storm a cavern she moved wearily
through, drifts hardened across the road, antelope stumbling
behind thin white lines of fence, and clustered cattle scoured
white, and round bales curled tight in their winter fur.
The road's curves she knew by heart, the baby not fussing
anymore, but quiet from something the doctor gave her,
and later, lying on the floor beside the crib, listening to
the phlegm in her small chest, she thought of fragile things:
moss, spiders' webs, lungs, the finch in hawk's talons
and the sky a snow of feathers on a day that had gone
till afternoon without a death. And in the night,
wakened to stillness, the wind died, stars, in the room
only her daughter's fluttered breathing, and *light* —
in the mirror, on the walls. She rose, went to the window,

and it was as if she'd found herself inside the pulsing
body of the world. And saw in the field her three horses
chase each other — the flown snow, the three circling
muzzle to tail in a kind of dance: rose-flecked, necks arched,
unspeakable — blood rushing in the stung
cold, the baby's cry, and their risen breath.

Woman's work

You've strapped the babies in the car and just need
to get to town, the snow having eaten through all the food
in the house, and stuttering over the cattle guard, look up
at the road suddenly filled with cattle moving their lumbering
bodies to another pasture, and you drive into the midst
of them at the speed of cattle, their big-snouted, innocent faces
peering in the windows, the babies staring back and pointing,
two men on horses guiding the herd. But you're thinking
about the cougar who took down another doe last night
behind the house, the dog barking all night, the doe's
hindquarters stripped to bone, the cougar hungry,
the doe too slow. And he, gone again; you can't move the carcass
by yourself, the cattle spilling over the sides of the road, sinking
their cloven tracks into the wet winter loam. You remember
how wild roses wove themselves between wires of the sorrow
fence, and the flattened rattlesnake the cows trample,
now glistening with mud and snow. But there is something
that wants to be born, a secret child eager for the world
with its predators and its wind and black hidden moon.
The babies bang pot lids in the kitchen at your feet, the house
with its scent of supper and unwashed diapers, and then
you're finally lying down, listening for cranes heading south
along the river, the silent breathing of sleep, when it is time
for the child no one knows, and you pull a scrap of paper
to yourself and begin: *the cougar hungry, the doe too slow,*
cattle spilling over the sides of the road.
Remember wild roses . . .

In any language

I cannot find the word in any language for *August,*
waning moon, when overnight the wind changes,
though there must be a word in Tlingit or Twi
for *when he left, his shadow went wandering,*
and would have been useful the day
I thought I'd found it — his shadow,
and would dry it on the line for him to pick up.
A reconciling gesture.
But it turned out that storm and water
had only shoved dry leaves against the shore.
Some things you see just aren't there,
like clouds that ride the river like a horse,
and some you can't see are as real as real, how
every night now grief sets a place at my table,
how a hawk's shadow once passed through me
and its secrets entered like a ship with folded masts
which unfolded once inside, like his fierce indicting stare
that still has not found its way out.
I could have used the past tense right then and there
for *overnight the wind changed.*
My body declares in the simple present, *Here I am,*
and goes on blinking my eyes, folding and unfolding my hands.
There must be a word in Mossi or Gan
for *I rebuke myself for waiting, knowing he'll never come.*
It might sound something like
                              let the great forgiveness begin.

Sacramento canyon

Can there be love spared of pity? Yes, yes . . . and I knew
when he told me, as we lay together in the sleigh bed, my head
a stone weighing down his chest, that he expected of me
nothing less. When it was time, he said. But the weeks passed
and he appeared perhaps stronger, though I may have but
dreamed it, *willed* it. He ate what I placed in front of him,
the lantern spilling its light and shadows, his form on the wall
grown giant, as the nights grew toward the close of the year.
Then the morning of silent snowfall, begun in the depths of sky.
I slept until a muted light filled the room, and wakened then,
and he was gone. As he had told me. His fate fulfilled,
the snow falling at a rate that rendered his tracks invisible.
I who knew him best, knew how he'd have gone — out beyond
the corral, the barn, past the sheep standing in their soiled wool.
He'd have taken himself into the canyon, and there,
and there . . . What is love? And what of pity? The array
of their disguises I had not considered until that moment.
And so willed myself to stay watching the white-flecked air
bury the fence rails, the ochre soil. And managed thus, a week,
until the snow baked down, until I called on Raúl,
and together, saddled his mules and descended the canyon,
and at some depth found him there, as if washed up
by a great sea, the woolen of his sweater, his socks
drawn into him as though they were, or willed themselves to be,
his own skin. And thought to myself that they too,
loved him, as I would have done the same.

East of the Rockies

The sky was noisy with rushing air like a river that's broken
through winter ice. And just about that cold. A rowdy sky,
the clouds herded down the valley. And hawks overhead
eyed us rocking in the bed of the truck, and the boss
who'd already made up his mind about me. But the cattle
with their peaceful faces, heifers, all pregnant, followed us
over furrows, the round bale in the truck pitching forward
and back, and the heifers shuffling along till the boss
hit the brake and we pushed the bale out, a thudded stillbirth.
The boss who called me Blondie, though my hair is copper.
He was certain my hair made me dumb. I have come
for the trial by fire, the refusal to deny myself. Feet numb,
we leapt out after the bale, air roaring, watering our eyes.
Cut the netting and rolled it out like a road.
A road made of summer laid over stubble and frost,
a road the heifers would eat up toward the coldest of the year,
their hides hanging ice, the earth bouldered in sleep.
The heifers all lined up for a piece of the road, each
to bear a calf come spring. And there I was, pregnant too.
Pushing the bale along. If I told the boss, he'd have fired me.
Already he figured I was worth squat. Was only waiting
for my cheque so I could quit. Dizzy, cold, hungry to the bone.
I tell you, the sky was loud that time of year.

Flying west

Strapped in our seats deep in the sky
through the window we could see our farm,
the shadow, a horse in the field.

And traced with a finger the river,
and remembered how it wandered
right past the house. Near dusk
we watched the yard light switch on.

One by one, stars flickered
in their distant yards. Trees
at the edges of fields grew dark.
For now, the haying would stop;
sheep would pour like a river into the barn.

That year we packed our things
and drove away, past the yard light,
the barn, though the house kept on
and the lilacs, the river, the grass.

Still, they whisper to each other
of what became of us, why we left.
I carry that farm like a poem
scratched on paper, tucked inside my chest.

Some nights I can hear the fox
padding along the cutbank there.
Some nights the dark
brings a letter from that place —

snow, it says, dust; the mare had her foal,
its new breath a wind
reaching far west across my skin.

Forgotten wars

Luanda, Angola

If we could close our eyes
and see the hidden.
We say, what happened, happened:

days, the miracle was born,
and went away hungry;
nights, the moon grew thin
and left with nothing in her arms.

There was rain, and the history of rain.
There was dust, and the history of dust.
These I rearrange.

The air said, for this moment
I will hold your steel, your impossible
weight, your wings.

The radio said, *whisky, oscar, lima.*
Five boys stepped on a land mine.
Come and get them.

The blown grasses said,
I drop anchor in this arid sea.
I hold the veins of darkness.

The sand said, I am older than all of you.
I will erase the world
grain by grain.

And we, with the agreement we made with earth
not yet complete.

And the radio said, *whisky, oscar, lima.*
You may turn back now.
There is no need.

And the galaxy said,
oh, little blue boat,
my green dream,
my once, my perfect child.

Hilda

Later, the boys said they understood Stanley'd gone back
to the house to take a piss but maybe he'd just gone
back of the barn, him and the boys in the midst of chores,
and so nobody knows for sure if Stanley knew the house
was on fire and Hilda in it, slow and slurred from the bottles
she carted around in her laundry basket, but it was a stranger
driving by who run past the house, toward the milking
operation yelling, and it was Hilda's boys who come out
running, one going in with his shirt half over his face, the other
breaking a window and spraying water from a garden hose
onto the furniture, which they say was the wrong thing to do,
them boys just thinking to find their mother while Stanley he
hardly looked up, just kept on milking, and pretty soon,
but not soon enough, a fire truck pulls up and then another,
and that was all the town had, two trucks and having to come
all the way out to the farm, but God the moon on the snow
that Saskatchewan night was beautiful, and the water freezing
onto the house almost as soon as it hit, the snow melting
in a ring, always was a sorry old house, that rusted
Allis Chalmers sitting in the yard and Hilda planting flowers
on the seat every spring and a circle of petunias around
the wheels was the prettiest thing about that house,
and one of the men stood on the chimney spraying down
while the fire ate up that roof, and somehow word got out
over at the dance hall and they all drove out in their pickups
full of gussied-up people, the crowd growing by the minute,
and everyone asking if they got Hilda out yet, who was gonna
go in and drag Hilda out, and they say she melted like wax,
slumped in a heap between the laundry basket and the door,
but Stanley he stayed with the cows till after the roof caved in
and the whole place was covered in ice, just smoke rising,
that house like a wounded animal that can't run no more
and sinks down finally, and dies.

When morning comes

When morning comes they'll burn my bones
and also my eyes, teeth, the delicate
                         furrows of my palms,
fed into God's wild mouth, rolled
into his sea of tongues
stretched out to swallow the small.
                         I, His coin, His moon
rubbed between finger and thumb
among His pockets' spider's web and down.

Brightly grasped was I, by God and by man,
and thus, chosen.

And of eternity's numberless ears, who could tell
                         my burst heart from birdsong,
the last of my breath
                         from the lint of dying stars?

Already the stories they make of me
                         stitch a fabric over the night
that will not tear.

I put my mouth to the earth and whisper
my innocence, my testimony
                         curled onto a snail's back
who carry the woe of the world.

When morning comes, I will lie inside my burning
as they say of me, *the book is closed.*

Now will you call me *enigma,* call me
winter, my teeth of ash, my tongue of coal.
                         I will become the wind's horses,
a seed's one wing falling, the first
crystal of snow burrowed in your hair.

– III –

Admonition

My husband warned me not to go out under the moon,
but once, I thought, could not hurt.
Thus I slipped from our bed while he slept, as moonlight
tugged at my nightgown, my hair, the tips of my fingers.
I descended the stairs like a silent milky light.
Outside, the moon sprawled over the snow
as I stood among the horses.
They had waited for me, they said, had taken
the long mane of my hair as a sign I was one of them.
The stars, too, widened their nostrils to learn my scent.
The wolf studied my tracks from the edge of the wood.
Thus I began, night after night, to go out in moonlight
and in snow to stand among horses. My husband
slept well and dreamed his hands shrivelled into paws,
his eyes grown small and round.
I carried no lantern, as the moon demanded of me,
and jealously commanded my presence as it folded its wings
onto the ravaged tip of the pine.
I stood inside the horses' breath, listened to their songs
and the moon's lonely mating call, unanswered.
Only then did I return to him, my husband, who warned me.
Certain I was he did not know.
I slept the sleep of snow, drifted, deep,
while he wakened, returned to himself, the sheets
soiled with paw prints, the blanket strewn with feathers
the colour of the moon.

When the wild horse spoke

Guard a place for the stranger and the hunted,
                whether horse, human, mouse or rabbit.
Forget not to greet the dead who live among us
                        at the edges of the herd.
Among you must be chosen one to stand and watch,
                one for the time of light, one for the dark.
Make not a trail to the place of a death, else you summon
                the monster's ghost, howling like a wind.
If any of us dreams of ravens, the wide leaves may be eaten.
At dark-moon, bow your heads, for this night
                        marks the end of old-time.
At hoofprint moon, raise your heads, for this night
                        is the beginning of new-time.
The night of round-moon-on-snow is the holiest of nights.
Gather together so to pass these teachings to our young.
Wind remembers story.
                        Should you any part of it forget,
approach her at a moment when she is swishing her tail slightly,
                grazing among the new grasses.

Virga

She took it as a sign, how rain
in the distant sky never touched the ground.
She thought it a sign but didn't know how or why.
And there were other mysteries: the way time
stops even as it ticks on, how anything
might all of a sudden reverse course.
Or that a person can just disappear.
Near the Mexican border she slipped past
the wooden doors of San Xavier del Bac,
and in the stone air lit a candle
for one who was dying. She knew
the wax would burn down, the wick
be consumed. She had travelled all this way
to witness rain almost reach the earth
but then rise, the way the soul leaves the body,
the way the body weighs less after death,
the way rain rises past the sky,
past anything the eyes can see.

Wild rose

The rains had come. The rains had come at last, and cattle
rambled in long, slow lines toward the barn. The rains
and dusk's stain spreading into what only yesterday was light.
She thought of June, June rain in the late light, and the evening
she came upon the bone house of a hare the ravens had dropped
into the horses' trough, the flesh ravaged by their beaks
and the water closed over it like a wound. And then
the whole lovely summer, and now the rains,
the mutinous leaves abandoning ship and flying, bright flags
in unmistakable surrender. She hiked up the wooded hill
through bracken, over logs moss-covered and trees spilling
their waters over her, wanting to find the place
where the twin bucks bedded down, Queen Anne's Lace
curled like the knuckles of a bird fallen in the grass.
Once, her lover took her to find the old farmstead at the edge
of a field, wheat scraping the air, though all that remained
was the cellar, a mouth open to the night, container for leaves
in autumn, *and snow so high you could walk straight across
and not know it was beneath you,* he said. She tried to take
it in, the nothing left of the house and its lives but wind
through vanished windows, the windmill banging its broken
wings. The way a house, and the life there disappears.
In rain she stood at the top of the hill, the firs parted
and distance spilling through, how last night she found
the moon again, a vague brightness in the clouds
like an old man's failing sight. *And when the snow melts,
the cellar is a pond, alone in a field, carrying the moon.*
And when they drove away, they took nothing with them
of that place, not even the wild rose and its unspeakable beauty
blossoming pale in the frail grass.

None so prized

The chickadee tells me
her singing is forgotten by the world
soon as it flies from her tongue,
comes to rest on a ledge of the wind,

then tumbles down the narrow corridors
between time and eternity.
Time can't hold it; eternity
slips it forever into his pocket.

The song is ancient, says the bird,
older than praise, younger than light,
cousin to regret, sister to fate,
the visible and invisible,

the tongue a bud yet to flower,
her singing weightless as shadow,
a droplet of water which turns
the world upside down —
cloud, cedar, bird —

a small inland sea the wind is greedy for,
hunger wind's motive, feather
leaf, seed and rain, all objects of wind's desire
but none so prized as a bird's song:
its mission to call all hearers to beauty,
a bell to awaken the day.

Listen, cries the song.
How fragile we are, how temporal,
secreted away in eternity's palm.

September

She wants somehow to slow the days, but knows it is as futile
as holding light, the cat mewling on the porch, all night
out hunting and now only loneliness between her paws.
How each night the moon climbs the firs and sails away;
the light impatient for going, even her lover flown
over the world and part of herself gone with him.
She waits at the window for a man to arrive with a shovel
and an iris, how she wants him to be her father, but can't
bring herself to tell him. She thinks instead of the long iris
leaves come winter, brittle with ice, and the ice shattering
into her gloved hands. Plums in a yellow bowl,
spiders weaving the last light at the corners of the house.
The robin who rode the summer out on the horse's back
has gone, and the siskin perched on the field gate takes flight.
Rivers run underground, unseen, the way desire moves
inside her, the days drifting by as if on a current.
And darkness has come from a far, far country to settle in
with his trunk filled with frozen mice and snow.
When the man drives up the lane in his truck,
he will plant the iris while she leads the horses in from the field,
the trees casting off their possessions to live like gnarled monks,
and the barn, the fence posts, shaping themselves for darkness.
Look how they roll their shadows out, she tells him,
and he looks up. And when he drives away, the shovel clanging,
she'll say, *for this moment he was my father,*
she'll say, *remember, remember by heart* the river,
sunlight in the canyon like manna she could almost taste,
and in the valley, the fields' yellow blossom,
machines cutting hay, the wild horses' gaze,
as if she could hold it all in her cupped hands before
the magician wind slips it into his fist, and is gone.

Bottle tree

Those boys, and the stories they told. *Nettie,*
they chanted from her yard, *Nettie.* And her tree
which moved with a voice that seemed to speak aloud
what one only whispered in the dark. That tree
                              and those boys' hands
cupped around their eyes at her window.
And grew into men, those boys, and old Nettie
with skin you could see right through, Nettie
who on the dusty street squinted up at the sheriff
                              from her glassed-over eyes:
Roy, your brother's here in his burial suit, says you cheated him,
says you make it up to Rose and the girls,
Roy tilting back on his boot heels, blood
risen to his face, hand slid over his holster.
                    That tree all those years
clinking its bones together, night and the clouds
a wall keeping the stars out, those boys
grown to be men, walked in without knocking,
and Nettie in her nightgown, like a bride, her white hair
                              tumbling past her breasts.
And all the while they drove her to the river
she said, *that woman a yours, be a hard labour, cord*
wound round that baby's neck.
                    Men they were, but boys
who could not see at the last
her mouth which opened but did not speak.
That tree with its music, and the stories they told
still swarming their ears like bees.

Umbilical

I planted them — the shrivelled husks, little broken flutes
into the soil of that place beside the cutbank of the river,
under shadow of the butte, laid them into the dirt
of that country so to tie my children to the earth,
that they may not flee from me back to their heavenly palaces,
where wind does not lay waste the fields, where the world
does not lie frozen months on end. Certain I was they'd pack up
their tiny hearts and go, soon as they could open their eyes,
the lightning-struck tree out our front window, the river
ice-jammed, threatening flood. Tonight the moon is lost
behind the rain. I have seen her frozen to the slough,
fallen through great trees. I have found her drowning
in shallow water. In that country where I tended my newly
born, no rose would grow, neither petal nor thorn.
Snakeskin waved pale in the pale grass.
And what about the dust still clinging to our bones? And clouds
that raced the river down the valley? And the moon spilled
across the floor of that house, another of her vessels broken,
while I rocked one or the other struck with fever,
his soul gone wandering. But I had hobbled them
to the rocky soil, wind, ice, the animal hungers of that place.
When we packed our things and left, the cords remained.
Wild mint closed their thin fingers over them — a cradle,
a grave. And it may be the river washed over them one spring
and swept them away. Tonight I wait again
for the moon to have a face. Her collect of fine white dust.
The rain has taken the rose's last bloom, her petals bright shards
in mud. My children stayed this side of paradise, and grew.
I did what I could, and kept them mortal.
As any mother would do.

Rain

Scent of damp earth through an open window and she thinks
rain, lights a candle to the darkened afternoon, water steaming
for tea, and in her mind she returns to the flat-roofed adobe
of her childhood, a man driving a horse and wagon along
their street, a fragrance — rain, and she imagines memory
as a kind of museum, with sets of long, thin drawers
she opens slowly, examining each small thing: a photograph
of her and her sister in identical dresses, a shattered milk bottle
on linoleum, a bloodstained sock, eyelet lace, the man lifting her
onto the seat behind the horse and her wanting to go with him,
knowing her mother would look out the window and find her
gone. Wind, dry leaves plucked from the trees,
the tea in her cup staining the water the way a river
flows into the sea like the sash on a dress undone and flying,
like burial cloth over the sunken bones of whales and ships.
A voice eddying through a telephone announcing a death,
her mother, the wagon-man long dead, and the horse,
but alive in a room of the museum, high windows and light,
the wagon's splintered seat, the horse waiting on its stone feet
and the man opening his hands to lift her into the air.
In other drawers lies a white glove, a weighted absence
tied with ribbon to longing, the fossil of her handprint in dirt.
But she will not look on those today.
She returns to the wind undressing the trees,
the complication of spine and decay, and rain on the window
writing in a script she cannot understand.

Silence

She grazes the field beneath
a seaplane sputtering above the firs.
Others pass over — hawk, falcon —
but do not see her among the bowed
grasses, tufts of dandelion.
Yet the barbed wire knows her, and the bees
who grow hushed in her presence.
Deaf, blind, she wanders shyly
among the stiffened, the mortal
leaves. Only her bright heart
feels the way along the fence line,
a single hair of her mane left behind.

Mercy

The maple forgives the wind
for stealing her innumerable children
    and turning them into birds,
into sinew and wing
    as the apple forgives the earth
for drawing all her sisters to herself —

and the earth — see how the earth
forgives winter for turning her to bone,
water, stone,
    daring her to outlast eternity,
a room scarcely furnished of light

    where a curtain billows
like a stranger in a black coat
who sows sparrows to glean the ground
    which dusk forgives
on behalf of the stranger, the sparrows,

by turning the snow to stained glass
and by this act of dye and hue
    forgives everything,
a ritual the dawn repeats, exonerating the darkness
    for its very being, unchangeable,

each cold star a candle alone on a table,
a flame guttering in a window,
    who forgives the moon

her absence, black pupil of the night
an eye the light cannot find.
    Forgive the light

for seeing right inside us,
silent, heavy with meaning,
neither speaking nor whispering
nor listening,

and we, half ghost, half child, a pin-prick
of God
which feels like wind, earth, ice,
like stone, stain, like desire, like flame.

Theology

After all this time she still blamed herself
for things that were not her fault.
Certain images, for instance,
that turned up in her poems. And God
who arrives as fog, as crow, as thorn, as snow.
Like Penelope, she unravelled
her own poems at night; others she hid
where even she could not find them.
And God who grieves by turning himself to rain.
Forgiveness is hard but possible.
As barbed wire sprung from its fence post
scrapes the air, and the air walks around it.
And God who leaves and returns
as grass, rust, as egg, as moss. Of course
it was all about love. And God
who covers his face. Disguises himself
as sand, as worm, as root, as wind.

The roan mare

She goes out into the afternoon with a bridle in one hand
and a child in the other, wild mustard in the yard
high as her waist, coyotes asleep in the cool underground,
lilac blossoms hard and dark as censers beside the vacant house.
Standing on the corral fence, she climbs onto the roan mare,
the child in front of her holding a shock of mane in her fist,
the old mare's spine a ship that creaks beneath them,
and beyond the first gate, the coulee ploughed in rows, wheat
stubble now, the treeless hills gone brown, and she remembers
as though looking through a window, how she waited
for the child's birth, before her face became the child's, became
her lover's, and in her mind she sees the valley
she rides through whitened to winter, icicles sagging
the horses' manes, snow blinding the windows, a bird flown
into the chimney, trapped in the iron stove, and her reaching in
with her hands spread wide as wings, the bird desperate
as a heart, ash swirling like burnt snow. Dust clouds burst
from the mare's hooves, she dreams some nights her own dying
from the sorrow of fences, the river's milky freeze
and her leaving him in the bed to fall through into that
swift dark, the way children tire beyond caring and lie down
anywhere to sleep. No one can tell her how she'll bury
the mare, that a morning will come when she'll waken amazed,
the moon all night riding the sea, the sky
and the sky in standing water filled with petals, the wind's
wild blossoming. She'll remember then coyotes calling,
a language she almost understood, something about stars,
how the night flies straight out forever, past the hills,
beyond the moon's frozen stare.

Peace country

I

Nearly May and snow
holding to the north side of the barn, grass
sodden with melt, her boots soaked through.
And beside, an open shed tumbling out grey wood,
and the drowning-pond's treacherous ice
covering its own darkness, below the vista
of budded birch and fir, the barn windows
spilling their damp breath.

In the distance the coal cars humped down the tracks
where the land was slashed and sutured, a wound
that scared her more because she knew it was her life
refusing to heal. She thought finding him would be enough,
enough to declare she was his daughter, meaning acceptance,
a fact. But there was more she'd have to prove, and lay
on her back in the hay, inhaling its hay smell
while swallows mudded the walls of their houses
in expectation for the life to break open,
the small hard beaks' relentless tapping.

And she reckoned he thought in lamplit evenings how
a daughter was burden, a burlapped load. In a broken
piece of mirror she saw a torn girl,
a mustang without brand. *To belong* —
the age in him a solid thing, like wood, his years
heavy enough to lean on, but it might turn out
he'd drop her out back like an old sofa,
a life instantly simpler for the act, she pondered
while her fingers combed her hair like a mane.
She had chosen him, and waited.

A heart's all creaking doors and peeling paint
and rusted latches, windows staring in stunned wonder.
She'd do what she could — forgive herself her poverty
and knock, quiet, on his rattling door, listen
for his breathing inside, hands in his pockets,
and behind her the pond like a moon fallen to the grass
and spring working its slow determined will.

II

As the eagle pair carried twigs and fur to the blown top
of the pine, and rain turned to snow and back again
stitching grey sky to ground, the old man and girl
ate in silence his spare cooking, the hearth fire
spitting out its opinions, the slow earth hardening
only as the sun allowed.

The girl made up her mind she'd track the horse
he'd let go wild and once over supper he spoke enough
to say she could have it if she could catch it and so
spent her first spring in that place, following the horse
she guessed had a few years still in him, and thought
the same about the old man.

A horse who trusted no one and a man with so many
wounds in him, she knew when she lay in bed
watching moonlight pour over the splintered sill,
no girl could stitch them all shut. And the horse
she also approached in silence, how it grazed the field
with an eye on her while she inched closer by the day.

The old man too kept his good eye on her, a serious face
she'd brought from the no-place she came from.
Every dawn she walked among wormwood and ash
in search of the horse, a dun with raven mane, and knelt
in the lengthening grass, knotting a rope halter from scrap
as robins tugged at the soil and fireweed blossomed out of stone.

When not with the horse she was in the corral, nailing
the fallen boards back. The evening she waded halfway
into the creek, slipped the halter over the muzzle
and led the horse home, he saw her coming, the reflection
of sky and cloud covering his face in the window,
how she stood on a rail to mount, the flesh rippling

beneath her hands, the dark stripe down its spine
between her legs. Everywhere in that country, wild rose
tangled itself in barbed wire, and down where the creek
met the river, the canyon spilled its secrets.
She knew nothing else in that moment
but the great horse heart beating through its skin

and the first hesitant steps until she passed
his cracked hands laced together over the fence,
some lost life reborn in his face. And felt inside him
a broken place mending over, while the moon
started up the pine, the three of them together
in the late June light, breathing the untamed air.

III

The girl knew she would stay until she buried the old man,
and then maybe she'd move on, she thought, riding the horse
across the fields, dried flowers, the land asleep, how she
could hear the hills' wild breathing in the afternoon, the haze,
smoke in the air from fires up north. The horse snorted
and shook its head, spilling flies she rode through,
one hand on reins braided from baling twine,

and with the other traced the line of black that ran down
its spine. She'd stay to mend the curtains, brush cobwebs
from the windows, and later, grown older, her hair cropped,
the axe in her hands, swift, coming down on wood
from the careless pile, and him silent in shade, a rusted
chair, his used-up hands spotted with scars. In her mind
he would hear the axe's cough, the wind that slowed

with the sun's going, the train hauling its load through
the canyon, the pines throwing their thin silence down.
And in the kitchen she'd turn the calendar to another month,
shouting out the date for him as winter nagged the corners
of the house, and beyond the window, the horse with its tail
flying in black strands. Yes, she thought, she would stay until
the night like a blind pulled over his face,

until like a broken road he lay down, and she
alone again in the world. A bony girl staring out across a field.
And she would know, finally, what love was. And take
a lover then, lie naked on top of the sheets, her hand
on his chest, and tell him of the old man, how she stayed
and stayed. But she'd change the story just enough,
not wanting to give him that beauty. Not yet.

Saying instead, *I was a seed, a tattered thing*
fallen from the sky, a feather with wings.
Now I grow underground, a root, a ruin, a house,
grave and solemn as stone.

IV

Her loneliness said *return*, but by then the dam covered
the canyon with its dark cloth. Standing on the precipice,
she remembered everything: how once, she was a girl
who lay on her back in a barn, and the canyon filled with sky,
a sea whose fish were named sparrow, swallow, osprey, owl.
An old man opened his door and she walked in.

How the windows broke the sky into pieces. How daisies'
hard spines cracked the dirt, their faces peered over the sill.
The kitchen clock's two stiffened fingers. The tractor
whose colour the wind stole, its wheels filled with mice
and straw. Sparrow's tracks in snow. The pile of field stones.
And he, bitten thin by weather.

And she thought of the two hearts, horse and man,
buried under the new sea. The fractured steps
he stumbled down at the end. The moon, too, drowned.
Only its light rising from the water.
And if the old man was hungry or thirsty, he could tell no one
but the thousand mouths of stone. He, the night watchman
of his own small room, his pine box bed.

Each noon and night he'd left the fist of his napkin on the plate.
She listened for the hay fork standing by the barn, for the small
silent boats, birds, but could hear no song.
And wondered if fallen apples could rise like a question.

In the days that passed she dreamt herself underwater, curtains
billowing over her bed, the willow waving in the yard.
Back then, she thought they were poor. Then she remembered
how lilac bloomed among barbed wire.
Once, she was a girl.

– IV –

Blessed is the waiting

This primordial light
has not visited since the great temples
were born, this light and the ferns
                    bowing down.
Silent, leviathan, this light has come back.

I will ask it for stories.
I will ask it for birds.
I will ask for one I love to return.
This light with its many colours: mist, lament,
                and listening for the moon.

I have been with horses, their scent
on my hands a kind of light.
The gate fallen to the latch
                    another light.
Absence slips past with its shadow,
separating darkness from light.
                I will close my mouth,
leave my tongue to sleep in its chamber.
I will speak with my hands only,
            the way trees do,
the way ferns. Ancient,
as snails float on rivers of light,
as the grasses step aside for them,
holiest and most fragile of the dawn.

In ordinary time

As she was dying, minor deities, twin-winged, thin-legged,
flew about the room. Remember — you brought the children
to her. Among the tea cups, saucers, the table and chairs,
there was no fear. Sandwiches on a plate — no fear among them.
Yet the small birds fled and did not warm the day.
Sunlight on the wall a sentence you read over and over
without meaning. You turned to face your son and saw
that he was four again, and you, crawling out of the truck,
cursed the missionary driver, lifted your boy into your arms,
brushed the shattered glass from his hair. Still, you will need
to get past the teenage soldier with his Kalashnikov.
The day having begun in its terrible innocence.
And like the first person, you must walk then among
the commonest weeds, the dried, shriven leaves, misery's flesh.
Rename the world.

Defending darkness

after Zagajewsky

Yes, defending darkness, the depth of wells, etc.,
but also horses sleeping neck over back,
the cat turning over small clumps of grass
and the moon, scraped, bitten, scrubbed clean.

Defending loneliness

after Zagajewsky

Yes, defending loneliness, the dark night, etc.,
but also the stripped branch clinging to the leaf,
the moon lit by afternoon, and the forest trail
that drops you in a place you've never been.

Patience

The heart was still waiting for her cloak of light
as five birds rose into the air, as the day
flew into dusk. I was wondering why
I had to live separated from them, even though
the quiet and luminous ropes tied us
to each other, deeper than this one life,
beyond earth, oceans, or speech. Waiting
on the heart to finish her grief, I kept watch with her
for the cloak, the light to be given, the kind
that settles in after a storm, or which holds
before slipping away on winter afternoons,
or when the moon lies in pieces on the grass.

The fires

We were three: four if you count the child
born before her heart could hold its shiver. We were four;
eight if you include the dog and cats, ten if you count
the horses. We were eleven with birds of prey,
                                more if you let in the sparrows.
We were innumerable if you count the grass.

The eagle pair were first, and took up the lightning-struck tree
with their curdled, intimate talk, while we
circled the house, hosing down the roof, the barn,
                flush riot of tamaracks on the mountain light-burst,
the wind's stars falling brittle onto grass,
when a fox and her young arrived and pressed their tracks
                                into the river shallows, a hawk
like a watchful clock on the barn's wet cusp.

There are days we believe we are farthest from heaven.
The air singed our mouths, ash paled the baby's face,
and night when it came, lay its illuminated manuscript over us,
                                the child and her failed heart
growing in spaces the silence built between us, the nearest hills,
in photographs shut tight into drawers. And stranded
in our skin, awoke, the sun a low red moon, to find
the lion who prowled among the neighbour sheep
lapping the river. Over the hours a coyote,
                                then antelope, filtered down.
Small owls peered out from their cutbank burrows.

A day or more held in its claw that uneasy peace.
As we held it also inside the house.
                        But knew we could not last,
and carried our fires with us when we left.

Passage

She knows the owls' mating cries and conflation of wings,
the branches' solid dark, how she stayed until light failed,
then lay in her bed by the window while the moon flew
toward the stars and the owls' throated music carried her
into sleep. In the clearing she'd stood watching a bush plane
bright overhead where sun lit the clouds and tips of the pines.
Already light was shrinking away from doorways and cracks
in the barn walls. She wanted to ride the gelding up the ridge
once more before the rains, her hands dusting off the saddle
and raising it to his back, the meadow high with thistle
and Queen Anne's Lace, dry grasses the colour of fence posts,
the horse's tail brushing off flies, his chipped hooves knocking
against the cedar's hard roots. Later, winter and walking,
she'll pick up an antler fallen in the snow, from the buck
who watched her on summer evenings by the creek, a scrap
of barbed wire caught in his rack. She'll carry it home,
delicately, like a gift, that impossible tangle, summer
sleeping in the bone. And when her lover calls from over
the far curve of earth, she tells him of the owls,
but has no words for the wildness they planted inside her,
the change he'll find when he returns.
Once when she was drowning, she looked down on herself
from above, her hair swirled over her face, her body dark
underwater, and waking in hospital, wanting it all over again:
the weightlessness when she left her body, her arms
thin wings opening, almost breaking through.

The way things separate

Always in that high desert she saw herself, a child bareback
on a black horse, shuffling its slate-grey hooves between pinyon
and juniper, the farthest hills, the sun that later would fall open
like a stain. And the face that watched her from a barn window
was her face, and she alone inside the barn with its air,
its memory animal, the smells of urine and hay.
Say what you will: I've seen deer graze quiet among horses
and then just disappear for days on end, as the moon does.
But in that country known for its stillness, the horse, old,
dependable, will find the slope between hills
while kicking small stones into the stream, the sound
bright as tin bells in wind. She knows this, even though
the horse and child have gone beyond sight of the road
where she rides in a car, where she is thinking of the ways
things separate: a fork in a river, a house she once lived in
now bereft of furniture, the glass shot through and the windows
rife with scars, how night divides all things from their colours,
the day the ice broke up and the Flathead jammed like glass
on the linoleum the morning her mother walked out,
a milk-fed moon spread across the floor. She remembers
bending over it, the moon cold, a wetness clinging
to her fingers. And somewhere, she couldn't remember
where, or on which side of the border, was a stone rose,
lichen turning its petals pale green. Such a hard bloom,
she thought, and then a knot of sparrows startled into sky,
each a small darkness which would grow to become night,
shadow of all the world's broken vessels.

How delicate

Now as in the beginning,
dark and light remain sutured to each other.
We are not separate;
       we are crows, we are smoke rising
over the field's narrow spine, a barbed wire fence.
         How delicate it is — how like the nearly
illegible handwriting of the grass,
         or the night's heartbeat you can hear.
Yesterday I watched the fortune-teller lay down
one card at a time.
         Her voice broke the news gently.
She didn't need to — I know he's not coming back.
And I can't tell anymore which is dream and which is my life,
all my memories smeared
         as if left out in rain.
Now as in the beginning,
we set the story in motion with our grief,
     a story which refuses sleep.
The hours I stored in jars — oh, I was careful.
If only I'd known they'd grow wings,
         fill the air with their songs.
Today I found a curl of birch bark on the ground,
a lost scripture fallen from a height:
        Begin again the [   ]
        each new [   ] of the world.
Only a narrow bridge connects this life
to the next, the unspoken water beneath.
I wait for lilacs, all those little bells.

How it all turned out

I did go on in my life, without a father, without
a mother. It is futile to look at those who have them
and ask why. I went inside and dressed what I found
in a father suit, a mother dress.
Kind of fakey, but they would do.
                          I pulled out myself at four.
She knew her parents were lost, wandered
into the forest, lured by the witch.
It was like the searing pain when the frost-bitten hands
plunge into tepid water. After a time
the fingers begin to open. The hot pink petals.
Slowly, slowly, as they can hardly bear
their own beauty.

How to disappear

It is entirely possible to disappear.

Begin by saying little.
Speak so softly no one will hear,

your confidence smashed on the rocks,
pulled under with the tide.

Lie down in a ripe field of wheat
and stare into the cloudless sky.

Here you are in the universe, trailing at the end,
the long arm of an unassuming galaxy.

Disguise yourself as the fractal pattern of sand.
Become the colour of wind.

Now you may evaporate if you like,
slip into your own shadow, eclipse,

burrow into the under-down of owl,
be the cry that flies from its mouth.

Or squeeze into a drop of rain;
leave only a pockmark in the dust.

With your fingernail, slit open the dark.
Climb in. It's quiet inside.

Only the earth with her delicate ear
can hear you breathe in there.

Listen. Someone is calling; someone
over and over is calling your name.

Don't come out till you're ready.

Maddybenny Farm

The boy remembers — eight hundred sixty-seven steps
from the door of his mother's cottage — twenty-three steps
to the gate where his fingers find the latch and let him
through, where his ears catch the clink of iron fitting back
into iron as the boy executes a right turn and finds
with his stick and then his palm, the damp stone of the wall
as the horse pounds a hoof against the wall of its enclosure,
a sound like a shotgun fired into the sky. It does not yet hear
the boy's approach, and if it can quiet itself will sense
the scrape of wood against stone that winds toward the farm.
The horse, two months before, brought home from the war,
battle-rent, shell-scarred, any clapped hand or door slam
would set it off, some vision burrowed behind the eyes,
tunnelled into mind where machine guns clatter and great
steel birds drop their eggs and the dead rise and fall
and nothing within the animal brain can make it stop.
Led by rope and halter over the ruptured earth, tied
in the hold of a ship back to this farm, the horse useless
now — how fear enters an animal as a fly beats itself
against the inside of a milk bottle. What does memory weigh?
What does fear weigh? Now the stablehand cups his palms
to strike a match, and his face, his cigarette flare as though
dawn were rising at the edge of the world on this night
without a moon, as the whites of the horse's eyes glisten
in darkness. For the boy, night and day are both alike:
six hundred steps or a little more before the clock-like bones
deep inside the horse's ears detect his coming, as the stable-
hand, leaning against the stable door, legs outstretched
on the cobblestones, hears only the horse's breathing, imagines
clouds of mist risen at each exhaling, and the boy visible now
in the stablehand's lamp — eight hundred sixty-five,
eight hundred sixty-six, eight hundred sixty-seven —

how the small hands slide open the hasp, and the horse,
ears alert, and the boy with his hands spread over the mane,
the neck, the great flat bone of the face, and when
morning comes his mother will take the very steps
to find a calm descended over the stall, and the boy
like a foal new born, asleep in the straw.

Not a poet

The poems arrive wild and blind.
They tap at the window.
They pace the floor, tensile
their paws. I don't want to be a poet anymore.

To be marked by God to stand apart,
to bear witness, make account.

There you are at seven, alone in the attic,
Mother on the rampage again.
And the house with its mouth shut, uttering not a word.
You sit up in bed, remind yourself — she's dead.
                    You were a poet then, too.

Also, there are the terrible fires of dying suns.
And the burden of truth. Discipleship's cost.
The poems insist that you tell it.
Some I have buried, some swallowed,
                    but once stitched together,
the poems won't be undone.

Sorrow's bones grow luminous with the dawn.
And God, who smells like sea water, like iron, like human ash.
And the small birds that rise from the cathedrals of His hands.
My hands form only a broken cup.
Around me leaves lie remembering
                    their brief moment of flight.

They too once were poets.
Blessed are the broken in spirit.
Blessed are the broken.

The sorrel gelding

When I awoke, and returned to myself,
remembering who and where I was,
I slipped from bed and by flashlight
walked out in rain, wind ripping the leaves
from the trees, the birds hunched low
in their small boats of straw.
And found him under shelter in the field,
checked his fever, buckled tight
his winter blanket, and fed a mash
of medicinal powder and sweet feed,
then left him to the night.
Morning, the blown leaves flared
as I set out to look for him
who met me at the gate,
ready to participate in the new day,
and I thought how simple love can be
and what can be gained by stepping into the dark.

The stone girl

And now that summer has come unravelled,
I think she must be cold, the blood-bright leaves
balanced on her hair, the first snow just now thinking of falling,
the night fallen onto the girl, naked, knees slightly bent,
her arms covering her breasts.
Only the smallest of birds drink from her hands.
No one notices her. The girl is forgotten.
All around is dark and silent. The streets, the tired houses.
The unconcerned suns, their fires, keep a distance.
She feels the constellations of sparrows on her wrists,
but still her milky eyelids close, her shoulders slump.
Stone, the girl. Stone, the moon.
Stone, the pedestal from which she cannot stray.
As if some minor god had told her, *Thus far
shall you come into life and no farther.*
Where is her mother? I think she must be dead.
And her father — who knows? The girl is forgotten.
But the story does not end.
There is a poem inside the stone, in the girl,
in the grace between her locked fingers,
the lichen spread along her thighs, in the curve of her hips,
in her hair carved by the sharp stone tool of the moon.
The poem on her tongue and her tongue rusted in her mouth,
a single word which means, *Not with peace.*
Not with peace but a sword. Slowly,
slowly, her lips begin to part. See her eyes ignite.
Such effort to move through silence.
Then the first growling, guttural moan. Then the word.

Surviving

You are not what you were.
But still some nights you can hear the wild
horses high on the plateau, the echo,
hoof-pounded stone, while God
                   turned child again, plays dead
away in the filaments of air
somewhere between the hawk's nest and the sea.

All this time hidden parts of the self
have scratched their names on bits of paper,
gathered behind musty doors in the brain,
while you inquired of the air as to your future
and the silent house answered:
                             it is not for you to know.

O let me not turn away — bravado a language
you barely knew. As it grew before you like moss.
As it covered everything.
The wild horses watching the place
                    where the forest began.

Every night turns day into the past. Spent.
             As if nothing is impossible:
the delicate cracks, a softening, the breakup of ice.

Whisper again the names of things —
that feral apple at the edge of the wood,
the peregrine all night hunting the moon.
                 Now write your history of rain.
These words of sacrament: *surely goodness and mercy.*
            Goodness and mercy shall follow.
And the heart in its nest of bone, deepening its white down.

Sonata

From the beginning, a shore.
Boats in their moorings.
And much granted us: the colour
of the water, the sea lapping against the boats,
grasses nodding off among the sand.
We were young then, meaning
our souls were young.

I tell you, in those days there was singing.
Which split my heart open, which did not heal.

Many centuries now have passed.
The bells of dawn ring with a sound
like small wrens waking,
and I rise and gather into baskets
rain and moss, the choirs of loneliness.

And still my burst heart spilling itself
to the moon carrying her milk pail
over the arc of the morning,
to the old man with callused hands
blessing his blind flowers.

Walking across the field at dusk,
the music rises in me again,
untranslatable, at the edge
of everything I know.

Tell me of the past lives of light
and darkness. Tell me how time
turns over in its sleep, waking
to dawn and a woman carrying in her arms
the missing pieces of an old man's story.

Day is a gate, the sun a stone.
The hand is a withered blossom,
yet a fist finds its way to knock at a door.
There is no map, yet the child inside the woman
finds the way to her father's house.

And the fist knocking at the door is my fist.
And I am the woman, I am the child
who found the way to my father's house.

If he will open the door, I will praise
with my wren heart the leaf-strewn
burrows in his eyes, the bread and wine
locked in his chest.
Sacred, almost human,
the snow geese of the Manitou settle out of air,
their bellies lit whiter than snow.

She found the field was really a church
where someone, coming before, had painted
great canvases of Paradise,
and she lay on her back in the damp
green of it, and for a moment could not tell
whether she were looking down
on a marvellous sea, or looking up
and whether she saw a reflection
of beauty, or beauty itself.

And she wondered if she knew what love was.
Was it yearning, or grief, heaven or hell,
the pause or the word spoken?
That which bore the name love lived inside her,
which she also called her children, her lover,
her father, many plants and animals
and also stars.

And each of these she held in a kind of light:
her father's hands, her daughter's hair,
the back of her lover's neck, the horses' manes,
so that everything appeared as though
preserved over centuries, even as she knew
their lives were brief as grass.

✍

Ancient when we were born,
our shoulders ached from the oars
we pulled across the waters of heaven.

Are you a dream? I asked my father in a dream.
Where he was going, I could not go.

And God? Is he playing that child's game again,
hidden, waiting to be found?
When I sit down to play Mozart,
who is it walking past the house
who stops to listen?